Behind Her Smile

Poetry

by

Sabrina LaBord

Cover Design by Sabrina LaBord and Dwella Pope

Cover Photo by Dwella Pope

ISBN 978-0-6151-4895-3

Dedication

This book is dedicated in loving memory of my dear grandmother,

Lillie Mae "Miss Janie" Moody.

I miss you, Momma.

Acknowledgements

First, I must thank God for choosing me as a writing utensil for poetry. I truly believe all gifts and talents come from Him.

Secondly, thank you for purchasing and reading my very first published work. I hope you will enjoy its content and tell others about it.

"Thank you" to my wonderful husband, Nowlin for supporting my dreams. Babe, you are my light and my rock or as you put it, I'm the mouth and you're the muscle. I love you Babe.

I have to thank our sons; Nowlin, Nevin, Richard, and Roosevelt for being my biggest fans. You guys are the greatest.

"Thanks" to Yolanda for suggesting that I share my poetry and to Dwella for pushing me to publish my work.

Last but not least, a big ole "thank you" to my fellow poets of The Writers Block in Augusta, Georgia for the late night sessions, the encouragement, and the creative energies we continue to share.

Peace and blessings,

~Sabrina (poetically known as Snow Redd)

About the Author

Sabrina LaBord was born in Augusta, Georgia; the third of four sisters. Because she was the too light, almost white evidence of an affair, Sabrina was left in the care of her maternal grandmother, Lillie Mae Moody from the time she was just three months old. Her grandmother (Momma) became everything to her.

Sabrina learned at a young age how to put her thoughts and emotions on paper. Her grandmother's words were law-no what ifs, ands, buts, questions, nor explanations were allowed. To vent her frustrations, Sabrina would find a quiet corner and scream everything she dared not speak onto paper. Then she'd tear it into as many tiny pieces as she possibly could and get rid of the evidence so Momma wouldn't find out about it.

After losing her grandmother to cancer in the year 2000, Sabrina found herself writing poetry as a means to cope with the flood of emotions she experienced. She shared her poems with a close friend who suggested she 'do something' with them.

Today, she is a wife, mother, and a soldier in the United States Army. She continues to write and aspires to become a school teacher after retiring from military service.

Table of Contents

I. Hearts

II. Minds

III. Spirits

IV. Thoughts (Haiku)

V. Souls

Risen King

Let Him in Your Heart

Abide in Him

*69 to Heaven

Use Me Lord

God Make Me a Flower

Save Him

Deal with the Devil

VI. Beings

P.B.E.

Beautiful Black Woman

A Man's Wonderland

Behind Her Smile

VII. Poets

Introducing…Snow Redd

Poetry Is

Thank You (for Writers Block)

I Gotta Write

Open Mic Night

Interpretation

Chapter One

Hearts

For Your Love

I stood on the moon and wished on a star.

…and here you are.

I prayed to God in heaven and made my request.

When the Lord answered back, He sent me His best.

I napped on a cloud and dreamt of your love.

You came down to me on the wings of a dove.

We danced on the sea without getting wet,

Waltzed around dolphins, walked on starfish for steps.

We made snow angels on icebergs without getting cold.

The splendor of our love will never grow old.

It will always be flavored with the newness of Spring

And sprinkled with the happiness and comfort you bring

to my mind, my soul, and to my heart.

I'll love you forever. You and I will never part.

Your heart sings to mine like a robin in a tree.

The refrain-a special song written just for you and me.

We are a perfect pair. For me there is no other.

Your smile is like a rainbow; warm and bright with color.

I don't even need the sun with its golden rays,

As long as I have you for the rest of my days.

Signs

I prayed for a sign that would lead me to love,

Get my feet on solid ground and out of the mud.

I asked for a sign to show me the path

Of life that is paved with happiness and laughs.

I looked for a sign, but the only ones in sight

Were stop signs, danger ahead, caution, and red lights.

Refusing to slow down, I lost control and swerved

Around the bend of love and pain's dangerous curves.

Trust hitched a ride and caused me to collide with deceit.

I paid the price for that. A broken heart was my receipt.

I gave heartache a lift. It nearly sent me off a cliff.

I took a detour down memory lane

But all I found there was the remembrance of pain.

The sign posted there said "15-minute parking only"

So I ventured on my way still clueless and lonely.

I came to a crossroads and stood there alone.

Lo and behold, a sign that read: tow-away zone.

Moving right along…

Turn left or turn right?

You see, this is my plight.

I'm looking for love and affection

With no map and no direction.

I've yielded to temptation, but it was a dead end each time.

My parking meter's run out and I have not another dime.

Aimlessly wandering, driving with blinded eyes.

I think I'll park and give my legs a try.

I'll take a nature walk off the beaten path,

Take off my shoes and walk barefoot in the grass,

Listen to the birds and feel the sun on my face,

Move to the beat of my own drum, stroll at my own pace,

Splash in a water puddle and let my hair down,

Do cartwheels on the ground until my frown turns upside-down,

Run 'til I'm exhausted and feel I'm about to faint,

Rest on a park bench before I see the sign that reads: WET PAINT!

You Mean So Much to Me

Sometimes I cannot find words to express
Just how much you mean to me.
I will say you have touched my heart in a
Way no one else has.
Knowing you has been a joy and a pleasure,
But loving you has brought new found feelings
Of delight and happiness into my life.
Every now and then we meet great people
Who inspire us and leave an imprint of their
Existence in our minds.
I must say you are one of the great ones.
When I am with you I want for nothing else.

My Shining Star

A touch of your hand,
Your warm embrace,
The sweet, angelic smile upon your face,
Your caring ways, and your loving heart
Are the things I long for when we're apart.
I hold you dear and love you true
Only time and distance keep me from you.
I'll hold your love in unclenched fists
For in my heart I truly believe this:
Here and now I set you free
And the power of love will return you to me.
From across the miles your ray of light
Brings me warmth on cold, lonely nights.
Beautiful people deserve one another.
I'm honored my friend to also be your lover.
No empty promises, no shattered dreams
I will not offer you any of these.
I'll value our friendship come what may
And hope it will last forever and a day.
So with these words I offer you
A chance for a love that's pure and true.
The warmth of your smile, the sparkle in your eye,
The beauty within you that lights the night sky,
A beautiful spirit is what you are.
I thank God for you, my shining star.

The Kiss

Your eyes ask my eyes if your lips can kiss my lips.

Though my lips utter not a word, my eyes answer "yes".

I lose myself in your eyes; sometimes blue, sometimes green.

As I anticipate what is about to follow,

I succumb to the gentle brush of your hand against my cheek.

For the very first time, I taste the sweetness of your mouth and

Experience the softness of your lips.

I close my eyes and sink deeper into the moment.

I melt. My heart races and my flesh tingles.

Mmm…nice.

I lean in to experience you for a second time.

I look at you. You stare back at me.

I wonder what you see in the brownness of my eyes.

Do they reveal what I'm feeling?

Do they whisper my secret thoughts?

Silence.

The rhythm of your breathing sooths me.

I'm lost in this moment; breathing it in as my mind records

The precious details of our first kiss.

One Thousand Tongues

If I had one thousand tongues this is what they'd say:
"I love you, love you, love you in a very special way".
And if those tongues could whisper in the stillness of the night
They'd whisper tales of your sweet love with wonder and delight.
If those same tongues could sing a song in perfect harmony
The song would be as sweet as the love you've given me
If I had one thousand tongues that all the world could hear
They'd shout your name for all to know who it is that I hold dear.

Unchained Desires

You've opened the box that I had sealed.

Do you like what's revealed?

Are you ready for what's inside?

Can you keep with my stride?

Do you have what it takes to keep pace?

A caged animal you've released.

Think you can handle the beast?

Suppressed urges, Hormonal surges,

Teased...tempted,

No longer resisting.

Animalistic tendencies inside of me,

A ravenous tigress unleashed and set free.

Confined no longer to the boundaries of abstinence,

Free to explore the flip side of celibacy.

Unrestricted by guilt, Uninhibited by conscience,

Liberated from the moral scrutiny of womanness.

Hungry for pleasure; an appetite beyond measure.

Fuel this fire and be consumed by its flame.

The heat doesn't burn...only makes you yearn

For more of the same.

I want you so bad I can taste it.

Just give me your time and I promise not to waste it.

I want to feel your touch over every inch of me.

Being in your presence awakens my sexuality.

You make me feel free, liberated, and beautiful.

All I have to offer, I want to give to you.

Take my body and do with it what you will.

Your manly flesh inside of me is what I want to feel.

Freedom to explore…wanting you more and more.

Consumed with desire…you take me higher and higher.

You've opened the box. Now come inside.

And reap the benefits of my unchained desires.

Will You Wash My Hair?

Honey, will you do something for me?

No, not that….but it does sound tempting.

I want you to wash my hair.

I want to feel your tender love and care.

Cradle me in one arm while the water saturates my locks.

The temperature is perfect; not to cool, not too hot.

Squirt a little shampoo into your palm.

The smell soothes my senses. I feel so calm.

Massage my scalp with your strong man fingers.

Entangle them in my hair and let them linger

Behind my ears and along my neckline.

Just go slowly and take your time.

All my stress and all my pain

Are rinsed away with the suds down the drain.

And while you hold me safe from harm

Fill my ears with whispered words of charm.

Intimacy is more than naked bodies between sheets.

Its you washing my hair,

Me washing your feet.

It's a conversation where no one says a word.

We speak with our hearts and each one is heard.

It's the little things you do that make me love you more.

You are my king; the man that I adore.

Wrap a towel around my head now.

My hair is clean.

And place a kiss upon my forehead-your woman, your queen.

Let Me Wash Your Feet

Babe, I want to do something special for you.

No, not that…but it does sound tempting.

Come over here baby and have a seat.

Let your woman wash your feet.

I've prepared the water with scented salt crystals

To soothe your feet and tantalize your senses.

I'll roll your pants up to your knees.

I want to do this right. I always aim to please.

Wherever life takes you, your feet get there first.

They're there on your best days. They're there on your worst.

As I gently rub the tension away,

I'll take away with it the stress of your day.

Forget about work; fast-paced and hurried.

Relax your mind and let me wash away your worries.

At home, you're free public opinion.

Inside these walls, you are king of this dominion,

The champion of my heart, the lover of my soul.

With you, I share my life. With you, I want to grow old.

Now I'll massage your feet with oil.

You are my champion after all. To the victor go the spoils.

Place one foot here between my breasts

While I massage your leg to release the stress.

I'll knead away your pressures and any negativity.

I do this because I love you; to show how much you mean to me.

And when you're fully satisfied. I'll end with one thing more.

A special little kiss for each and every toe.

Reservation for Two

Welcome home baby. I have a surprise for you.

I've planned a special evening; reservation for two.

No kids, no phone. I don't mean to be rude.

I've dimmed the lights to help set the mood.

Let me take your jacket and help you with your belt.

'Cause I'm about to give you the best love you've ever felt.

We've got all night so we don't have to hurry.

And I'm in control tonight, so don't you worry.

Are you relaxed yet? Let me massage your back and feet.

Then I'll feed you strawberries —tender, juicy, and sweet.

Don't worry if the juice should run down your face.

I'll take care of it with my tongue as well as that other place.

I won't stop there. We're going to extremes.

I'll take my pleasure in your squirms and your screams.

Scream if you like it. Beg me for more.

We can start on the bed and move down to the floor.

We can do it on the counter or up against the wall.

We can make love in the shower and pretend it's a waterfall.

Make our way to the garden where no one can see.

I'll be the flower and you'll play the bee.

Two bodies in motion glistening with sweat.

And we've only just begun. We're not done yet.

Will you allow me to take my hand

And feel that thing that makes you a man?

Throbbing, pulsating with a heartbeat of its own.

Hot with desire like a fire full blown.

And then while up and down I slide

I'll gently squeeze you with my muscles inside.

I'll move real slow and take my time.

You'll know that I'm yours and I'll know that you're mine.

And when I'm done, you'll sleep like a babe

With reminiscent dreams of the love we've just made.

An Otis Kind of Love

"If I were the rainbow after the storm, I'd wrap you in my colors to keep you warm.
That's how strong my love is".　　　　*~Otis Redding*

Give me a love like that.

The kind that grabs hold and never looks back.

Give me love that's sweet and caring

Like the lyrics of a song by Otis Redding.

Try a little tenderness,

A warm and gentle caress.

Lose your sense of time

In these arms of mine.

I wonder if I sat on the *dock of the bay*

A man like Otis would happen my way.

He'd leave there whistling a different tune

Because I would make him my *love man* and soon

We'd make *dreams to remember*

January through December.

I'd have *pain in my heart*

Anytime we were apart.

You could call him *Mr. Pitiful* or even a *tramp*

But when it comes to love songs, even in death, Big O's a champ.

Big O, *I've been loving you too long.*

From a little bitty girl to a woman now grown

Duets with Carla Thomas,

Crooning expressions filled with promise.

Or grooving with the band

Makes me wanna get up and dance,

Put my hand on my hips,

And let my backbone slip. *Shake!*

Horns so sweet they could top pancakes.

Bring it on home to me.

I love it when you call me baby.

Can you love me like that? Is your love that strong?

Cause I'm just *lovey dovey* for an Otis Redding song.

Meant To Love

Our meeting was not by chance.

Nor was it by chance we grew to love one another.

I was meant to love you.

Yes, there have been loves in the past.

Through bad experiences and failed relationships,

Our eyes are opened that we may learn to recognize

A 'good thing' when it comes along.

You are my 'good thing'.

You possess qualities rarely packaged together:

Compassion, understanding, consideration,

Not to mention respect, honesty, and a great sense of humor.

You have been shaped and molded through your own personal

Experiences in order that you may recognize and appreciate

What I have to offer in this relationship.

Yes, I was meant to love you and to be loved by you.

A Prayer for Us

I went down on my knees today and prayed a special prayer.

I asked God to watch over you and keep you in His care.

I prayed that He would bless my heart to better love myself.

For I must master loving self before I can love someone else.

Although you're far away from me, I love you just the same.

I prayed for us and asked these things in His son Jesus' name.

Life's Treasures

There are some things more precious than silver or gold.

They live in the hearts of the young and the old.

I call them life's treasures 'cause they're precious indeed.

You can't buy, sell, or steal them so there's no need for greed.

A photograph that's captured a moment in time

To help me remember when our lives intertwined.

A single petal from the rose you gave on our first date

Pressed between the pages of a book to help create

A lasting memory of the time we shared that night.

Our first kiss as we held hands in the pale moonlight

To love and be loved is a treasure in itself

So don't be a fool and keep your love upon a shelf.

Love was meant to be shared through the hearts of mankind.

I remember the day I offered you mine.

These are the treasures I've been speaking of.

Life's treasures are the memories we make with the ones we love.

Tears of Loneliness

In the still of the night my heart cries out for you.
Silent tears blaze a trail from my face to the pillow.
I struggle to find peace and comfort in my own
Mind to shield me from the pain loneliness brings
When you are not here.
The smile that greets the morning sun fades away.
My brown eyes now sparkle with the bluest of tears.
I know it won't last always, but for now it
Gets me through each day.
Still to love you and miss you is far greater
Than to never have loved you at all.

One Day at a Time

Alone again I lay tonight
Holding my pillow, squeezing it tight.
My body yearns for the warmth of you
But again I'm lonely, sad, and blue.
I close my eyes and drift away
Back in time to an earlier day.
I'm there again, safe in your arms
Not a care in the world, no thoughts of harm.
Life is good again, full of meaning.
It seems so real although I'm only dreaming.
The light of day has come once again
Bringing my time with you to an end.
I'll meet you my love when the darkness falls
On this house, this bed, and these four walls.
I await the day I awaken anew
Having slept in the loving arms of you.
'Til that day comes I'll be just fine
Missing you one day at a time.

Another Day

Another day has come and gone.
Another day you're away from home.
Another day my arms are empty.
Another day wishing you were with me.
Another day wanting your touch
And thinking how I miss you so much.
Another day closer to your return
It's the positive approach that I have learned.
Another day to think of you
And all the wonderful things you do.
Another day to appreciate
You, for whom I've decided to wait.

Reminders

Your picture in a frame
The mention of your name
The scent of your cologne
At night when I'm alone
The candle that I light
Each and every night
The song on the radio
By Joe, "I Wanna Know"
The beach where we held hands
And walked together in the sand
Everywhere I go and everything I do
There's always something to remind me of you

You Say

You say you love me, but you won't.

You say you want me, but you don't.

You say you need me, but you don't show it.

You say I mean the world to you, but I don't know it.

You say you can please me, but you tease me.

You say you'll always be here, and then you leave me.

You say… You say…

Meanwhile, I'm slipping away.

Where I'm itchin' you're not scratchin'.

No more words. Please just show me.

Take the time to tend my needs.

I need action. Satisfaction.

Promises are nothing if left unfulfilled.

Like dreams smothered, extinguished, or killed.

You're killing me without knowing it.

Stop saying you love me and start showing it.

You say… You say…

I say….I've heard enough!

Walking Shoes

Oh you might get me down but
I promise you won't keep me there.
Like my momma used to say:
"I can do bad by myself".
If I was strong enough to stand by you
I can certainly stand on my own two feet.
See when you were trying to pull
Me down you made your own hole deep.
I let you back me into the closet of my mind
With your cussin' and fussin'
Always putting me down.
I stayed there a while lost and confused
Taking your mess, being used and abused.
But I'm coming out stronger than before.
I have a made up mind and my hand is on the door.
You see I keep up on a shelf
Deep inside myself
A pair of walking shoes.
I'm through singing the blues.
I'm walking right out on you and I won't look back.
I'm walking out of here proud, strong, and that's that!
You say I've changed, but you've got it all wrong.
I have a new attitude and a brand new song.
No more singing the blues.
It must be the shoes!

Chapter Two

Minds

Angry

You need to get angry.

Yes. You need to get angry.

Maybe if you get angry, you'll get off your ass.

Hell. Get too angry!

That's a double dose

And some of us need it most.

Some angry is what you need

To turn your words into deeds.

You need to get angry.

Yes. You need to get angry.

You think Martin Luther King didn't get angry?

He was dragged off the bus

And put in hand cuffs.

He got angry!

He was put in jail

And had to post bail.

He got angry!

Yes, he was non-violent,

But he was not silent. There's a difference.

He got angry!

He boycott the bus,

Spoke up and made a fuss,

Held sit-ins and stayed,

Got on his knees and he prayed.

He marched and he spoke.

Congressmen and presidents he wrote.

He got angry!...and he got results.

Do you think master got a case of niceness and turned his slaves loose?

Hell naw!

They got angry!

Black men, women, and children (some of them his).

They got angry!

Working in the heat and

Their backs beaten,

Their babies stolen,

Their feet and ankles swollen,

Hell yeah they got angry!

They were shackled and chained.

The rebellious slain

Their blistered field hands,

Far from their homeland

Packed in ships,

The crack of Master's whip,

Their women raped,

They had to escape.

You damn right they got angry!

Harriet Tubman got angry.

They got angry. They got the Underground Railroad.

They got angry and some of them hung

From trees by their necks they swung,

But as a people they got angry and they got freedom!

So what gets you angry?

Don't sit on your thumbs and look dumb.

Get angry!

Stop complaining, waiting for someone else to fix your problems.

Get angry!

Get bothered!

Get angry!

Get too angry!

That's a double dose

And some of us need it most.

Some angry is what we need

To turn our words into deeds.

Get angry! Get busy.

Get angry! Get an education.

Get angry! Stop feeling sorry for yourself.

Get angry! Get a job.

Get angry! Get that no good so-and-so out of your house.

Get angry! Get it together.

Get angry! Stay angry—until you get results!

How Proud

Ribbons of blue, red, and white

Bows of yellow to guide your flight

How proud we are of all you've done.

We await your return dear daughter, dear son.

A candle in the window and earnest prayer,

How proud we are of what you've done there.

Because you are on watch, in freedom we rest.

Welcome home brave soldier. You've given your best.

Reality Check

Reality TV.

Remember when talk shows were just that?

What are we saying?

Now all we see on the tube

Are women flashing their boobs,

Daughters fighting their mothers,

And every one's got a secret for another.

Jerry! Jerry!

Uh uh.

Who told you that was cute?

And grandma's on the pole in her birthday suit.

I'm trying to figure out where America went wrong.

Let's take a commercial break and bring the psychiatrists on.

Talk about our problems and get to the root of the fruit of our pain.

Exploit us not for the sake of ratings.

Get your hooks out of the ghetto and quit baiting

My people with calamity disguised as glamour.

And Ricki Lake…

Could she be more fake?

Go Ricki! Go Ricki!

Please! Standing there flipping her hair

And pretending to care.

"Cheaters busted."

I'm disgusted.

Who are you helping?

She knew he was cheating before you brought them on your show.

Now that her dignity has dissolved,

What have you solved?

Shh--. Quiet on the set.

Her self esteem is low.

So right back to him she'll go.

A wasted trip; still ill-equipped

To escape her dilemma or even realize she's in one.

Networks are pimps and judges have become hoes

On street corners in the form of court shows.

You rush home from work to catch it.

Judge Judy, Maybelline, Joe Brown, and Hatchett.

Where's the justice in that?

That being the fact that they dishonor the bench

Just to get a pinch

Of tainted fame and glory.

Cut! Let's rewrite the script. We need a new story.

Maury wants to know "Who's Ya Daddy?"

It's your business being splattered.

Meanwhile, his pockets are getting fatter

With blood money.

DNA stained dollars.

You see a free paternity test.

What I see is a demoralized mess.

A dirty picture;

One painted with the mistakes and the pain from our lives.

Twisted and distorted images of our realities,

Smudged with the ugliness of lies and deceit.

Shame and hurt portrayed as humor.

We may as well be in black face.

Who's laughing now?

Just because they say it's free don't make it free.

Are you willing to pay with your self-respect and your dignity?

That is the price.

Who benefits? Who profits?

Not you. You're just today's topic.

Will Montel shed a tear for you when the cameras stop rolling?

When your heart is still hurting, your eyes red and swollen?

Will he call to check on you months after the show?

Not just for an update episode, but because he genuinely wants to know?

We'll answer that and other questions after the break…

Like milk left out too long, that which could have been good has now curdled.

Its foul stench makes me heave and hurl.

America's been hypnotized.

Take the blinders off her eyes.

See things for what they really are.

Talk show drama won't make you a star.

Be a star in your own light.

Don't contribute to our people's plight.

Be an example to future generations.

Stop living down to society's expectations.

That's not my reality.

Neither should it be yours.

Make better choices.

Have something to say when you lift your voices.

Rolling in 5…4…3…2…

Mic check...check one…check two.

Reality check…check me…check you!

Happy New Year

Out with the old and in with the new,

A new year unfolds for me and for you.

A brand new beginning, the past year behind.

Hope for the future in every heart, every mind.

I wish you prosperity and lots of good cheer.

From a friend to a friend, have a Happy New Year!

Untitled

We met at eighteen. At twenty we were married.

Three years later, your first-born I carried.

You said you'd be whole with me as your wife.

But now you needed a son to complete your life.

You were right there with me for every appointment.

Little did I know there'd be great disappointment.

Along came our son, as perfect as could be.

Your attention quickly turned to him and you began neglecting me.

"He looks just like his daddy" you said. And that was all that mattered.

You didn't seem to notice my breaking heart as it shattered.

Insatiable is the word that describes you best.

The strength of our marriage was put to the test.

I've given you my all and all. I don't know what else to do.

You tell me "I've got my boy now. I don't need you."

First came the neglect and now the disrespect.

You used me, abused me, and took me for granted.

I've reached my threshold. I can no longer stand it.

The arguments and fights,

The tears I shed at night.

We're twenty-four years old now, contemplating divorce.

You decided you'd steer all our lives on a completely different course.

Intentionally (and without my consent) you planted another seed.

Said it was because "a playmate is what our boy needs".

Very clever, but I know better.

You didn't love me, but you didn't want to let me go.

Where were you this time when my belly began to show?

No back rubs nor massages, no display of paternal pride.

I rode this one out alone and it was alone that I cried.

You and I turned twenty-five before our second son was birthed.

You already treated me badly, but him you'd treat much worse.

He didn't have his father's eyes. To you, his tone wasn't right.

It was me who had to give him love by day as well as night.

You wouldn't even hold him, nor sing a nursery rhyme.

You chose a favorite of our two sons and to him you gave your time.

"He doesn't look like me" you said. "We don't yet have a bond".

Neither did he look like me, but I knew he was my son.

I learned to smile through the pain you caused. I learned to hide it well.

I refused to let our baby boy be subjected to all that hell.

Resentment set in and hatred followed to replace my pain and tears.

With just the boys, I walked away from the man I'd loved nine years.

You soon realized all too late what a wonderful thing you had.

The son you rejected, with each passing day looks more and more like dad.

We're twenty-seven and the marriage has ended.

You want to have it back and mend it.

"Too little, too late" is all I can say.

We each have to go our separate way.

You can't have me so you neglect your sons.

The boys you wanted so much, yes those are the ones.

Little to nothing in financial provisions, a phone call here and there.

They need and want their daddy's love, but you don't seem to care.

Broken promises and disappointment are all you send their way.

It's gotten so they don't believe a single word you say.

How can a father forget his sons and disregard his responsibility?

It takes a mother and a father in the process of fertility.

Both are responsible (in case you somehow forgot).

A mother, I am. A father, I am not.

You should see how much they've grown; our precious little ones.

Maybe you'll come to your senses and be a father to your sons.

It's Not Over

Through centuries of struggle and many years of strife
They fought and died to give me a better life.
A life of freedom with rights and respect
Let us all remember and never neglect
To pay tribute to those who helped freedom ring
The Harriet Tubmans, the Malcolm Xs, and the Martin Luther Kings.
Let us not forget the ones who made it all happen
The Rosa Parks', Sojourner Truths, and the Reverend Jessie Jacksons.
Black History Month is the time we commemorate what they've done,
But the battle's not over, the war not yet won.
Prejudice still dwells in the hearts of some,
But like the old spiritual – we shall overcome!

Nobody's Perfect (for Sara)

I know that nobody's perfect.

I guess that's why the one person we'd walk

Through fire for is called a best friend and not

A perfect friend.

We were inseparable, you and I.

We said we'd be best friends 'til death.

Something happened along the way to change that.

I began to doubt the one person I had trusted with

My tears, my fears, and things I'd never

Tell another living soul.

Even when I gave you the opportunity to come clean,

Still you lied to me.

You should already know that I accept you

For who you are.

I only wish you could be the friend I thought you were.

One Final Request

Don't give me no wake. I'm trying to sleep.

It just costs more anyway and you know I'm cheap.

Give me a simple funeral; a song and a prayer.

It's fine with me having all of you there.

Don't make up my face with all that paint

Trying to make me look like something I ain't.

A plain white gown is all I need

And please not one with those puffy sleeves.

No necklace, no earrings, no jewelry at all.

Keep all that stuff back here with y'all.

An old wooden box will do the trick

And a hole in the ground; two feet by six.

Now that I'm prepared for my eternal rest,

I have but one last and final request.

You can lean over to give me a hug and a kiss

Or whisper in my ear how much I'll be missed.

But don't you cry in my casket!

If you insist on boo-hooing, bring a hanky to catch it.

Chapter Three

Spirits

Sweet Lillie Mae

A sweeter name I'll never know

Nor see a face with a brighter glow.

I'll never hear a voice so kind

Nor touch softer hair turned gray with time.

You took my tiny hand in yours

And filled my life with so much love.

A mother like you is special indeed

For stepping in when a child's in need.

I always saw you proud and strong

And then one day God called you home.

We always had great times together.

I guess I assumed you'd live forever.

Today, tomorrow, each and every day

I will remember you, my sweet Lillie Mae.

In Loving Memory of My Grandmother, Mrs. Lillie Mae Moody
March 27, 1921 – July 27, 2000

Wisdom on My Sleeve

As we stroll arm in arm, I'm on a mental walk through

the fields of my dreams and the meadows of my memories.

I recall the stories, the lessons, the blessings, and all that you've taught me.

The seams of my moral foundation were hand-crafted by you.

I remember the tales you told of those who were sold…of winters so cold

and how I came to be in the fold.

I am but a leaf on a limb of a branch that is rooted in you.

I was carved from the bark of your tree.

That's how I came to be.

I am proud to be fruit of your fruit and seed of your seed.

So today I walk with wisdom on my sleeve.

Every silver strand of your hair makes you lovelier and dearer.

Your testament, growing pains, heart aches, back aches, sweat,

blood, and tears bring me nearer.

Nearer to your struggles and the lessons you learned from your mother…

Your younger years working the cotton fields, and how you made it through.

Nearer to that five mile walk to school one-way each day with a hole in the sole
of your shoe.

You taught me that life's a journey and not a race.

And so today I am conscious to keep a slow and steady pace,

Pull my shoulders back and I smile as a smile graces your face.

And when that day comes for you to leave,

My heart will surely grieve,

But I'll be thankful for time well spent. The time you invested in me

and the person that I have come to be.

Thankful for all the knowledge that school and college couldn't teach me.

It was your words of wisdom and encouragement that reached me.

As we stroll arm in arm, I walk with wisdom on my sleeve.

Mothers Love

No love on earth can compare to that which
A mother has for her child.
From the very beginning a bond is established
Which can never be broken.
No matter how old the child grows or what path
She chooses in life,
A mother's love will be there to the very end.
It comes in many forms – sweet and tender
Or stern and unyielding.
It nourishes, it teaches, it protects, and it heals,
But it never fades nor does it ever die.
A mother's love is special.
Bless them for all they do.

Welcome To the World

No greater love have I ever known,

Than that I have for you sweet child of my own.

Within me you grew into a perfect little being.

And now for the first time its Mommy you're seeing.

I vow to you on this day of your birth

To nurture, love, and teach you all that you're worth.

My greatest achievement I hold in my arms.

I will help you grow and protect you from harm.

I see in your face a reflection of me.

And in your eyes a look of uncertainty

Rest now my child; you've come a long way.

And welcome to the world on this, your birth day.

For All The Times

For all the times I told you to wait.

For all the times I had to work late.

For all the times you didn't understand

Why I made you wash your hands.

For all the times I scolded you.

For something I told you not to do.

For the toy you wanted that I could not buy.

For all the times you asked me 'why'.

Today we'll spend some quality time.

I'll put all other things out of my mind.

I'll listen to you and the things you like.

I'll even help you ride your bike.

I'll view the world through your eyes today

And while you sleep tonight I'll pray.

I'll ask the Lord to help me please

Be the mommy that my son needs.

Remind me of the role I play

In how he'll turn out someday.

This day is set aside for you and I.

I love you, my son - the apple of my eye.

Sisters

We did not choose one another.

It was written in the stars.

There's beauty and strength in a love such as ours.

Flesh of the same flesh, born of the same blood

Nothing can come between our sisterhood.

Through good times and bad,

The hurt and the tears,

The laughter and joy we've shared through the years.

You are my sister and I love you dear.

I am your sister, when you need me I am here.

God's Gracious Gift

(written on the occasion of Major General Janet A. Hicks' retirement from the Army)

The Hebrew name, Janet means "God's gracious gift".

How fortunate we are to have had you in our midst.

Elaine is French and it means "light".

To follow your guiding beacon, has been our delight.

You are one of a kind; a rare and precious find.

Your warrior's spirit and strong shoulders,

Coupled with an undying commitment to soldiers,

The heart of a woman and a mother's warm voice,

These virtues combined made you the logical choice

To lead, to challenge, to nurture, and to build.

Generous and compassionate of your own free will

For your seeds of generosity,

You shall reap reciprocity.

Always getting to know people; not just their names.

From Private to General, you value soldiers the same.

A defender of nations, protector of the meek,

Your fidelity and vigilance never sleep.

You're genuine in every way;

Sincere in word and deed,

Fulfilling every promise, meeting every need.

For your service to our nation,

We will forever be grateful.

For the lessons we have learned,

These honors come well earned.

As you enter now into your retirement years,

We'll be watching through bitter-sweet tears.

Bitter to lose the jewel that we have found in you,

Sweet to think of all that you're still yet to do.

Decades from now, through the Signal Corps Halls of Fame,

Will be heard echoes of your name.

With a distinguished career of many firsts and great success,

We thank you for sacrificing your absolute best.

Not wanting to let you go,

We proudly deem you "hero".

This salute we proudly lift

To "God's gracious gift".

One of His best picks…

Major General Janet A. Hicks

A New Beginning

(written on the occasion of Command Sergeant Major Reuben Peppers' retirement from the Army)

As one chapter in life closes, a new one begins without missing a beat-
Recording precious moments; each milestone and every feat.
Continually written before the ink has dried,
Pages of emotion; the somber and joyous tears cried.
Line after line for one so well traveled,
Bound by God's sheathing; never to be unraveled.
Protected by His grace, deserving of His favor,
He keeps in His care, His dedicated laborers.
Volumes of distinction, honor, and sacrifice,
Defender of our Nation-preserving our way of life,
Giving of yourself with the sweat of your own brow,
Accepting every challenge-never asking why?...or how?
Lay down your armor warrior. Faithfully you have served.
Today, we salute you as you so greatly deserve.
As we bid you farewell, don't think this is an ending.
Your story is still being written. It's only a new beginning.

Cultural Uplift

Change is inevitable.

It's neither bad nor good.

Or is it?

Change…evolution….different; yet

Holding on to subtle likenesses.

We need change as much as the gravitational pull

That keeps us rooted and grounded.

Roots.

Running, growing, intertwining, and overlapping.

All things old are made new again.

Fingers which once mushed collards and hot water cornbread

Into a perfectly blended mouthful now clasp forks.

The same pot of greens, the same cake of bread.

Not the same taste, we've diluted the flavor.

Bell-bottomed pants and platforms.

Same concept, a new generation…a new spin.

When did 'change' change for the worst?

Was it when the rent money started coming from

Not daddy's but mama's purse?

Or was it when our sons' underwear became outerwear?

Or when grooming our daughters' minds became

Less important than grooming their nails and hair?

A cultural upheaval.

Let's get back to the basics.

Back to pressing combs

And family Bible studies at home.

Back to hide-and-seek

Not who packs the most heat.

Rent parties and chastisement from the lady down the street.

Another whipping when you get home.

A cultural uprising.

Change.

Uplift and maintain those positive traditions.

Uplift your brother.

Uplift one another.

Cultivate culture.

Embrace it.

Uplift and maintain those positive traditions.

Father Unknown

Thank you my father whom I've never known.
I wonder about you still even now that I'm grown.
Am I at all like you? Would I have made you proud?
I thank you in my heart since I'll never thank you aloud.
I've searched and I've prayed to find you someday,
But from me your identity is still kept at bay.
Whether conceived in love, lust, or in shame
I think I deserve to at least know your name.
To look upon your face and maybe compare
The tone of our skin, the texture of our hair
I neither judge you nor my mother for your sins
I only wish I could know the other half of my kin.
To know you would help me know more about me
For it was your seed that created half of my being.
No heritage to pass on to the generations to come
'Cause the line was cut off before I was born.
You missed my first steps and graduation day,
But I thank you for my very existence anyway.
Maybe we've met or passed on the street.
I hope I was kind if we ever did speak.
I hope I was smiling and standing up tall.
I just wish I could have known you – that's all.

Chitty Chitty Bang Bang

Chitty Chitty Bang Bang walking down the street

Jumping into cars with every guy she meets.

Ooh she looks so fine,

But there's one thing on their minds.

She meets an older guy

And she thinks he's so fly.

Chitty screams no! But he just hits it harder.

For the rest of her life, now he has scarred her.

Chitty Chitty Bang Bang walking down the street.

Her belly is so big she cannot see her feet.

Chitty is so round,

But daddy can't be found.

Her mama should have schooled her.

That man would not have fooled her.

Chitty and her baby walking down the street.

Daddy's in jail 'cause Chitty's fourteen.

Don't grow up too fast and give away your ass.

You are a precious pearl.

Please just be a little girl.

Belief Without Color

Belief without color is ignorance in a cloak…stale fragments of a life unlived.

For life is vibrant and jumping with color!

Hues of blues from water to sky.

Tides of crimson blood, royal bloodlines, and the sweat of brazen warriors.

Without belief in self, one will never attain true wealth.

Not "money green". I mean the wealth of discovering a lineage derived from earth tones. Dust, clay…chosen, shaped, formed, and molded to be the original man. Nostrils flared by the breath of God Himself. Commanded to procreate; not dissipate. Commanded to be commander of a land rich and flourishing with rare flowers and cool waters gushing forth; lakes spilling into rivers and rivers running to the oceans blue.

Bearded lions and wooly lambs roamed the plains in harmony. Black and white stripes ran freely beside enormous grey beasts with ivory tusks through fields of golden brown wheat and lush evergreen forests. Now, black and white stripes are painted on the backs of men confined by grey cinder blocks because they don't believe they were predestined to achieve greatness. Belief without color is hopeless.

Stale! (Laziness and procrastination)

Pale! (Conformed to a doomed society)

Drab! (Stripped of its original essence)

Belief without color is a bland pot of gumbo cheaply made. Watered down…

Substitutions for this and omissions of that…tainted with bad ingredients…too many hands stirring the rue.

Be reborn of color! Reclaim it. Own it. Be painted a believer.

Repaint me with the regal colors of my forefathers.

Color me with hope. Color me happy. Recolor my hair nappy.

Paint my toes thick and black-brown; tough from running barefoot on the ground.

Paint hands clapping and toes tapping.

Drum beats vibrating my chest while I dance beneath the orange moon.

Brush my tongue with words of respect and admiration for my elders.

Draw my ears big enough to channel their wisdom.

Touch up the corners of my mind with a sponge. Make it absorbent; ever expanding and increasing with a constant thirst for knowledge. For we believe knowledge is power so without it, we are…powerless.

Pour buckets of brotherly love and compassion in my heart to flush out the residue of hatred.

Spill the full spectrum of the rainbow into my spirit. Illuminate me.

Belief without color is null.

Belief without color is death and damnation.

Help to resuscitate a dying nation.

Embrace it. Dare to dream, reach, and explore.

Study history and her story and their story…mine and yours.

Belief without color is fruitless.

A tree which bears no fruit is cut down.

Belief without color is…………..not our destiny!

Chapter Four

Thoughts (Haiku)

Haiku #12

Thunder and lightning,
Splashes of rain ease my pain
Like an orgasm.

Haiku #16

The heat in my loins,
The rise and fall of my chest,
Anticipation.

Haiku #19

The birds and the bees,
Humming birds and buzzing toys,
Nature's orchestra.

Haiku #73

Raindrops, come quickly!
Splish, splash, veil my teary eyes.
Hide my quiet storm.

Haiku #11

Temptation and lust,
Baited; hook, line, and sinker.
Infidelity.

Haiku #27

Washing over me;
Flooding my ears with laughter,
Watching children play.

Chapter Five

Souls

Risen King

I don't know how you feel,

But I know God is real.

My hands have not touched nor have my eyes seen

Yet still I know Christ is the risen King.

By His disciples and followers He was loved and adorn.

Disowned, crucified, His flesh ripped and torn

With fish and bread, multitudes He fed.

Mocked, ridiculed, thorns pressed into His head

He came to this world to save the lost.

He was beaten mercilessly. That was the cost.

He healed the sick and made the lame walk.

He suffered and died for not His, but our faults.

He gave peace to the grief stricken, down trodden, and broken hearted.

He was pierced through His side, spit on, poked, and prodded.

He calmed the winds and walked on the sea.

He endured stakes driven through His flesh for you and me.

Blameless and perfect, He took on our sins

As they pounded and hammered again and again.

He took one final breath, with a heavy heart He sighed.

Jesus lowered His tear-filled eyes, hung His head and He died.

He's the only man ever born from a virgin's womb.

His broken body was wrapped and laid in a tomb.

One day, two days, three days His friends cried

But on that third day, the rock was moved aside.

Where was His corps? Was it stolen by a thief?

Who would want to bring His mourners more grief?

Grieve not my friends

Because that's not how it ends.

He walked out of that grave and to Heaven ascended.

He's been to hell and back-the keys apprehended.

He shook the bowels of hell and set the captive free.

He put the devil in his place and gave us a permanent victory!

What He did for us was an honorable thing.

So honor Him always, Jesus Christ, the risen King.

Let Him in Your Heart

Can you hear Him knocking?

Will you receive Him today?

He stands at the door of your heart and He's not going away.

He's patient and loving. He's waiting on you.

So tell me, brothers and sisters what will you do?

Swing wide the doors of your heart.

Allow Him to dwell there and never depart.

Hold fast to He who alone can make you whole.

Hold fast with your heart, mind, and soul.

Make your body a willing vessel to be used in His plan.

He won't abandon you. He'll hold you by the hand.

When the waves and the current become seemingly too rough

He'll carry you for He knows when you've taken enough.

He knows your heart and how much it can bear

'Cause remember – you allowed Him in to live there.

Abide in Him

When your so-called friends are gone
And you feel like you're all alone
He's been there all the while.
Because you are still His child
You need to worry not
But just in case you forgot
He's waiting patiently
To break the bonds of iniquity.
You don't have to fear
Just rest assured He's always near.
God is always by your side.
In Him you must abide.
Depend on Him. Have faith.
He'll strengthen you to run the race.
Cling to His bosom and your soul shall be fed.
He'll place the spirit of peace upon your head.
Trust in Him forever more.
Into your heart comfort He will pour.
Abide in Him and never doubt.
Only He can bring you out.
Out of darkness and into the light.
You are precious in His sight.
In all things, allow Him to be your guide.
In Him you must abide.

*69 to Heaven

Hello? Jesus! I'm sorry I missed your call.

You see I was just too busy to answer. That's all.

I stopped to take a peak at the caller I.D.

So I knew it was You who was calling me.

Yes I know you're never too busy when I call on You.

Lord there were just so many things I needed to do.

I tried to do them without You and now they're all out of whack.

That's sorta the reason I *69'd You back.

So tell me Lord. I'll do what you say.

And please forgive me for ignoring You that day.

Oh Jesus, thank You for taking my call.

I accept this task and I'll give it my all.

You're the only one on whom I know I can depend.

And that is because you're my one unfailing friend.

The phone is ringing.

Will you answer?

Use Me Lord

Use me Lord in your master plan.
I come before You with outstretched hands.
I'm pleading Lord, begging You please.
I humble myself before You down on my knees.
May all my deeds be pleasing in Thy sight.
I'm fixed on You, God my guiding light.
Oh Prince of Peace, Ruler of all things
What peace and joy to my heart You bring.
Teach me your ways God. That's what I need.
My soul belongs to You. I'm free indeed!
Without You I am nothing. With You I can achieve
Any and all things as long as I believe.
Use me Lord Jesus. Put my feet to the fire.
To love You and know You is my heart's desire.
I submit myself Lord. You have total control.
I neither fear nor fret because I know You're on patrol.

God Make Me a Flower

You made me a delicate flower,
But that flower wilted and died.
A cactus grew in its place, made tough
And stubborn with pride.
A flower's petals hold the morning dew
To rinse it clean with beauty anew.
A cactus holds its moisture inside,
Never to be seen 'til that cactus has died.
God make me a flower, delicate and sweet.
Take away my armor of thorns and plant my feet
In soft, rich earth that I may once again shine
With the dew of the morning on these petals of mine.
God soften my heart turned hard through the years,
That I may be refreshed and cleansed by my tears.

Save Him

Dear God, it's me again.

This time I'm praying not for me, but for my man.

He's gentle and caring with a heart of gold

But Lord I need you to save his soul.

I make my request in Jesus' name

Hoping the man I've chosen and whom You've

Chosen for me are one in the same.

I've bound the devil to withdraw his evil spirit.

Father send your Word that his ears might hear it.

I, like him was once lost in sin

But I cried out to Jesus and He took me in.

My soul's been cleansed. I'm covered by the Blood.

And now my Lord I want you to save my love.

I'm claiming that he's saved according to Acts 16:31

and standing on faith that its already done.

I know that You will save him for I've made my decree.

I just hope that You'll save him and give him to me.

Even if You save him and yoke him with another,

I thank you for answering my prayer and I'll love him as my brother.

Christ loved us and for us He died.

We'd never make it without You, I know because I've tried.

Thank You for listening. I know You understand.

I just had to ask You, "Lord please save this man".

Deal With the Devil

There's not much to it. It's simple you see.

He's bothered me many times, so take it from me.

If some fool on the street was babbling in your ear

Telling you all sorts of things you didn't care to hear,

You'd be quick to call him a liar

Or give him a look that could burn like fire.

The devil's no different. Do him the same way!

Open your mouth and this is what you say.

(And don't be ashamed to call him by name.)

Devil you're no good.

I'd slap you if I could!

What you're sellin' I ain't buyin'

So you're wastin' your time tryin'.

Why should I accept your five-minute fame

Then burn forever in hell's eternal flame?

You talk of fame and glory

But you never tell the whole story.

Jesus never lies.

He couldn't if He tried.

You can't give me what He can.

He's got all power in His hands!

Are you still here? Get off my back!

Or I'll call my Jesus. And you don't want that!

Can't you see that I'm saved?

I refuse to be your slave!

I tell you what you can do.

Sit down a minute and let me witness to you.

Oh now you want to flee.

He can save you too just like He saved me.

What? You don't want to hear it?

Now you know how I feel you wicked, evil spirit!

That's right, run! Get on somewhere and hide.

I'm a Christian full of faith so where I go I walk with pride.

You're nothing but a trickster, a hustler, a low down sneaky snake,

A liar, a phony, you're just a big fat fake!

But you never give up, so I know you'll be back.

And next time I ain't gonna cut you no slack!

You've been rebuked and I've been redeemed.

Jesus and me make an unbeatable team.

Chile that's all you gotta do to get the devil out your path.

'Cause he don't want no parts of my God's wrath!

For that fool on the street you might need some mace.

But to fight off the devil just arm yourself with faith!

Chapter Six

Beings

P.B.E. (Pretty Brown Eyes)

With the ability to entrance,

They are a platform for light to dance.

Welcoming and inviting...

Seductive and enticing...

Two sparkling copper pennies-their worth unparalleled.

Your gaze is bought and paid for; to stare, you feel compelled.

Gentle and caring,

Fiery when they're glaring.

Not long do they stay that way.

They tell what my soul has to say.

Look closely and you may be surprised

At what you see in my pretty brown eyes.

Beautiful, Black Woman

Whether permed or natural,

She's got it going on.

She's black. She's beautiful like

A queen on a throne.

The brownest of eyes,

The thickest of thighs,

The fullest of lips,

The curves of her hips

Whether paper bag brown or pecan tan,

Deep dark chocolate or milk chocolate

On the other hand.

It's in the way she walks.

It's in the way she talks.

She's feisty as hell if you get on her nerves

With her hands on her hips to accent her curves.

She knows how to dress

When she wants to impress.

She's got a style that's unique

From the weave in her hair to her pedicured feet.

No matter her size, shape, or shade

She's got it made.

She's a beautiful, black woman!

A Man's Wonderland

Your face is like the sunrise; bright and glowing.

With your smile, you warm me up inside without knowing.

Two stars for eyes, they twinkle with wonder

Captivating me as if your spell I'm under.

Your voice, a gentle whisper in the wind,

Resounding in my ears again and again.

Your lips are the moon; full and round.

One kiss can send my rocket soaring.

One more can bring it down.

That is only the face of your earth, but there I cannot stop.

Your body's a wonderland with two big mountain tops.

Their perfect peaks make my knees weak.

I lose my words and cannot speak.

Your valley is my favorite place to play.

I can play in the valley all day.

From its thirst-quenching river I sip,

While brushing the river banks with my lips.

Cause an earthquake sending tremors to your core.

When that quake ends, make it tremor twice more.

In your waters I sail my ship,

With my hands anchored firmly on your hips.

And when my voyage comes to an end,

Slowly, I climb your mountains again.

I bury my head in nature's chest.

And there I'll slumber in sweet, sweet rest.

You are my earth; magnificently created.

Your beauty is one which cannot be debated.

I'll explore your circumference three sixty degrees

Discovering all its hidden pleasure possibilities.

Behind Her Smile

There was a nice young woman whom many adored.
But what was really behind the beautiful smile she wore?
She had pretty brown eyes, soft and friendly.
But it was her radiant smile that I mostly remember.
It lit up a room; cast out darkness and gloom.
Pleasant and cheerful; it gave peace to the fearful.
She kept an arsenal of smiles for passers-by,
Usually accompanied by a "hello" or "hi".
Never once did I see her frown.
Surely, she too must at some time be down.
How could one woman's face hold so much delight?
Her face probably smiled while she slept at night.
That beautiful smile was quite a sight to see.
I automatically smiled back when she flashed it toward me.
Her cheeks would plump and her eyes would crinkle.
The corners of her mouth bore laugh lines and tiny wrinkles.
I'd like to secretly spend a day amidst her thoughts.
Walk around inside her mind without being caught.
What would I discover there....any disappointment or pain?
Would I like what I found there?
What knowledge could I gain?
Does she get angry or lonely, depressed, or blue?
When she smiles on the outside, is her heart smiling too?
Where has life taken her? Was the road paved with strife?
I'd leaf through her memories to reveal the story of her life.
If I could walk in her shoes for just a mile,
Maybe I'd uncover the truth behind her smile.

Chapter Seven

Poets

Introducing...Snow Redd

Forget Snow White. I'm Snow Redd.

Don't scratch ya head. You heard what I said.

And please-

If you hafta write it down, spell my name with two Ds.

Snow Redd.

Augusta, Gee Ay is where I was born and bred.

I was fat back, grits, and collard greens fed.

And that's where the flesh will be put to rest when I'm dead.

I'm a southern chick with a spirit that's free

and a knack for poetry.

SNOW...act like ya know.

She's the girl in me who likes to have fun.

Well rounded but still got corners like an octagon.

My friends say if I was white, I'd be a blonde.

REDD...yeah that's what I said.

Likes to make reservations

and hit you with sensations

you never felt before.

'Cause my lyrics are hot to the core.

Learn the name.

One touch of my flame

keeps you coming for more.

I burn my words into your brain and leave my stain.

Like the sun and the rain, I bring the pleasure and the pain.

I keep it real.

I speak what I feel.

SNOW REDD.

Get it in your head.

'Cause I'll be spittin' poetic flames until I'm dead.

I'm Snow Redd.

Poetry Is…

It's a piece of me.

It's a work of art.

Written expressions that come from the heart.

What's within, must come out.

That's what poetry's all about.

An outlet to some, a hobby to others,

Loving words to describe your mother,

The words of a love song, a greeting card,

A diary entry you'll never discard,

A rappers rhyme; words set to time,

An old school beat with new words meet.

When your voice is heard

It's spoken word.

Onto paper you pour your spirit

In the form of meticulously chosen lyrics.

Poetry is life. It's blood from a pen.

Birthed from a spark of inspiration.

It reaches minds. It touches souls.

Poetry broken hearts consoles.

Wordsmiths perform the ceremony

That unites pen and paper in matrimony.

A haiku, a limerick, it could be one verse.

Sometimes poetry's at its best when life is at its worst.

We put it on paper to lighten the load.

And those who've been through it can decipher our code.

Poetry is you. Poetry is me.

Poetry is the result of our emotional debris.

Poetry is…

Thank You (for the Poets of Writers Block)

Thank you for lifting the veil and encouraging me to broaden my horizons;

To see past the limitations I'd put on my potential for growth.

Thank you for teaching me that the setting of the sun is not the end.

For as sure as it sets on this day, it will surely rise and set again tomorrow.

A new dawning brings another chance, new opportunities, and new ideas.

Thank you for pushing me to the edge of the earth,

So I could realize that it is multi-dimensional and not flat.

Thank you for being a willing participant in the slaying of my fears-fear of trying…fear of failing.

Thank you for the strength in you pulling at the strength in me…

Helping me be reborn out of confusion into destiny…into my destiny.

Thank you for pushing me harder and harder 'til I fell, but even more for being there to help me to my feet with the realization that I have a gift, a talent, a destiny…

To experience life and paint it with words that others may experience my falls, my highs and my lows, my feats and my woes without ever leaving the pages of a book.

Thank you…for painting your pictures with your words that I might see what lies in me.

I Gotta Write!

Gotta write…gotta write…anything…something…(sigh) Nothing!

One can't write without thinking and all I'm thinking is-*I can't write!*

You see, it's not like stage fright because stage fright is fear

Of that much, I'm clear and I'm not afraid to write. Oh no!

 I welcome it, beckon it, call it near to me, and hold it dear to me.

I love to write. To me, the absence of writing is sin!

Putting thoughts down with pen again and again…

I love to breathe it in. It's like air when my mind's up there…

Like home when I'm in the zone…

Just wanna be left alone when I'm emptying my dome.

Now what?

Not a spark of inspiration in sight.

"Say brother, can I get a light"?

Now you understand my plight?

I just gotta write!

Like whipping a dead horse, it can't be forced or coerced.

It doesn't have to be factual but it does have to come natural.

Like on those sleepless nights when I gotta turn on a light and write, write, write

Until those bottled up thoughts are poured out onto paper…

Until the lead breaks and my fingers ache.

Until the pen runs dry and the page is damp

And I catch a neck cramp, but I can't stop!

Writing revising, flowing, going, rhyming, perfecting the timing,

Pouring out my spirit, painting images with lyrics.

I live it, I need it, I feed it and it feeds me.

I crave it. I'm a slave to it. I wreak of it. I sleep next to it.

It's my pleasure, my treasure, my passion, my poison…

It's my gift and my curse. *If I could just finish this one verse!*

It's my prison, my freedom of expression, written record of my life's lessons…

It's my voice, my sight, my sound… Like wide-ruled, it's got me bound.

I just gotta write!

Open Mic Night

It's open mic night in this smoky coffee house.

Whereas, it should be as quiet as a mouse…

You disrespect my rhetoric.

I've got a microphone and you're louder than me.

If you want me to continue, then respect my poetry.

You see, my words are an art form and deserve your attention.

So put your mouth in time out before I put you in detention.

Or should I come sit next to you for my words to get to you?

I came here to share my craft and be heard.

Apparently, you came to hear some spoken word.

So…why don't you shut up and listen!

Thank you. ☺

Interpretation

Its a gift with the power to mend a rift…

The rain in me, the sun in you,

A morning glory opening to the fresh fallen dew,

Picturesque words, thought-provoking images,

Adjectives, adverbs…invoking one's feelings,

Pen to paper, mind to voice,

Metered, sporadic, your style, your choice.

A poet may be divinely gifted.

But by what instrument is talent to be sifted?

Flour through a strainer is soft and refined.

Those grains that remain can be so too with time.

Cast out prematurely; discarded too soon…

A bud weeded out before its opportunity to bloom.

Style, technique, flavor, a slick beat…

Anticipation, then evaluation of the enunciation equals interpretation.

I sincerely hope you've enjoyed reading my book and that you will tell others about it.

Alas, I leave you with this thought-

Smiling is highly contagious. Let's start an epidemic! ☺

Visit me on the web at:

www.myspace.com/snowredd

www.ingramcontent.com/pod-product-compliance
Lightning Source LLC
Chambersburg PA
CBHW031002090426
42737CB00008B/645